Helping People with Developmental Disabilities Mourn

Mourn

Practical Rituals for Caregivers

Marc A. Markell, Ph.D.
Foreword by Alan D. Wolfelt, Ph.D.

*Companion Press is dedicated to the education and
support of both the bereaved and bereavement caregivers.*

*We believe that those who companion the bereaved by walking with
them as they journey in grief have a wondrous opportunity: to help
others embrace and grow through grief—and to lead fuller, more
deeply-lived lives themselves because of this important ministry.*

Companion
P R E S S

For a complete catalog and
ordering information, write or call:

Companion Press
The Center for Loss and Life Transition
3735 Broken Bow Road
Fort Collins, CO 80526
(970) 226-6050
www.centerforloss.com

Companion Press is an imprint of the Center for Loss and Life Transition,
3735 Broken Bow Road, Fort Collins, Colorado 80526

Companion Press books may be purchased in bulk for sales promotions, pre-
miums or fundraisers. Please contact the publisher at the above address for
more information.

Printed in the United States of America

14 13 12 11 10 09 08 07 06 05   5 4 3 2 1

ISBN: 1-879651-46-7

To the two loves of my life, Ed and Eli, who teach me what it is to live well and love well everyday, and to my sister and dear friend Katie for all her love and support throughout my life

Foreword

This practical, user-friendly resource meets an important need in the art of caregiving to people with developmental disabilities. I often say, "When words are inadequate, have ritual." All too often in our efforts to help bereaved people with developmental disabilities, we rely on "talk" therapy. Many people assume that when a person with developmental disabilities appears "normal," normal means of communication will be effective. However, we often find that meaningful rituals are a much more effective means of support and care for grieving people with developmental disabilities.

I cannot think of anyone more qualified in this area of grief care than Marc Markell. His years of experience in "companioning" people with developmental disabilities shines through in the pages that follow. This heartfelt book is a must-read for anyone who wants to "walk with" and compassionately support grieving people with developmental disabilities. It is packed full of easy to understand, easy to use rituals that will help you help others. Marc provides sensitive insights and practical rituals for helping this under-served and often overlooked population.

Alan D. Wolfelt

Preface

People with developmental disabilities are diverse and unique; they are similar to and different from people without disabilities and each other. I have had the honor of working with and teaching individuals with developmental disabilities at the secondary level, in a summer park and recreation program, and in group home settings for almost 30 years. I have worked with and supported people with disabilities from preschool through adulthood. Every age and every situation has given me opportunities for growth in the understanding and appreciation of the unique gifts people with disabilities can offer.

Now, as a college professor in a department of special education, I continue to work directly with individuals with disabilities as well as educate future teachers of individuals with special needs. This, too, is a privilege. I have the chance to influence teachers to help their students live as independently as possible with full and emotionally healthy lives.

The examples included in this book are either from personal experience, events I have observed with the teachers and student teachers I work with, events I have heard about from students or workshop participants, or created representations of how the ritual might be used. The names of the individuals with disabilities and facilitators have been changed. Even though some information is fictitious, the examples have been written as close to what actually happened (or what could happen) as possible.

Acknowledgments
I would like to acknowledge the people with developmental disabilities whom I have had the honor of learning from throughout my life; Alan Wolfelt for his support and all I have learned from him; Edward Breun and Kathryn Markell for their support; and Karla Oceanak, for her kind editorial guidance.

About the terminology in this book

"Individual with a developmental disability"—a child, adolescent or adult with mild, moderate, severe, or profound developmental disabilities. Others may refer to developmental disability as mental retardation, mentally handicapped, or cognitively impaired.

Levels of developmental disability—Generally, the levels of severity for a person with a developmental disability are defined by IQ test scores:

- mild (an IQ of 50-70)
- moderate (an IQ of 35-49)
- severe (an IQ of 20-34)
- profound (an IQ of <20)

However, as with any system of categorizing people, this cannot capture any specific person. We are not able to tell a lot about what a person is capable of doing or who the person is by an IQ score. The categories are helpful, however, in a general understanding of the severity of the disability. In the examples used throughout this book, when I use a category to describe a person, I will explain in more detail the capabilities of the unique individual.

"Person who died"—a significant person who has died in the life of an individual with development disabilities, such as a parent, sibling, friend, classmate, room- or housemate, teacher, paraprofessional, care staff, or any other significant person in the individual's life.

"Facilitator"—a parent, teacher, paraprofessional group home staff or any other care provider who may be facilitating a ritual.

Introduction

While grieving the loss of a significant person in our lives, many of us participate in—and are helped in our healing process by—the use of ritual. Some of these rituals come in the form of funerals or memorial services, which usually have similar and often familiar characteristics. Other times, rituals are uniquely created for a person or a group of people to help heal a loss.

Ritual has been very broadly defined depending on the purpose of the ritual; however, typically a ritual includes some element of symbolism. This symbolism represents something beyond the actual event or activity of the ritual. The symbol used in a ritual may represent some aspect of a "higher power," but does not need to.

Whether traditional or uniquely created, rituals are most often geared toward people without disabilities. In fact, about 15 percent of individuals with developmental disabilities are not even included in any type of grief ritual after the death of a significant person. Even when they are included, they may only be peripherally included. They may be physically present, but little if any effort is made to involve them in a meaningful way. As a result, they are often forgotten and disenfranchised mourners.

Not only are people with developmental disabilities often excluded from meaningful ritual, they are often lied to or told half-truths about the fact of the death itself. The thinking goes that inaccurate information will pacify or protect them. Some of the inaccurate information is of the same type that adults give to children when someone loved dies, such as the person who died is "sleeping" or "God took him because he was so good." Another reason that others in the disabled person's life resort to euphemisms is that they may be uncomfortable with the topic of death and don't want to talk openly about it. As with children who are told untruths when someone loved dies, people with developmental disabilities may act on the information in unhealthy and self-destructive ways. They may fear falling asleep or they may act-out with inappropriate behavior in an attempt to not be "good" so they can stay alive.

Yet being outsiders to death rituals does not mean that individuals with developmental disabilities do not grieve; they certainly do. And because they grieve, they need opportunities to mourn. They need opportunities to participate and heal from rituals—rituals specifically created to meet their unique needs.

I have had the privilege of teaching classes on grief and loss at the graduate level for teachers and group home staff working with people with disabilities. Many times the students and I discuss how we, as facilitators, can create rituals for individuals with disabilities after the death of a significant person in their lives. I find that my students are often somewhat at a loss for ideas about what types of rituals could be helpful and healing for people with disabilities. This "being at a loss for ideas" seems to be one of the obstacles that prevents facilitators from creating and conducting rituals. They may ask themselves, "How do I even start?" Without a starting point, rituals will not happen.

Even though all people are different and there is no "one way" to create ritual for all people with disabilities, there are certainly some common characteristics of people with developmental disabilities that need to be recognized and addressed when creating such ritual.

Because of the nature of their disability, people with developmental disabilities generally need more concrete experiences in order to participate fully in ritual. They also tend to need fairly explicit directions and simplified activities. Rituals that are abstract or open-ended may be confusing, frustrating, and of little value to them, yet it's also important to maintain an element of symbolism.

Creating effective rituals can be especially challenging for people who are nonverbal or have limited verbal and cognitive abilities—yet it is certainly not impossible. The facilitators of such rituals not only need to be very deliberate and cognizant of unique needs, they also need to facilitate participation in the ritual experience.

This book contains 20 different death rituals—from the very concrete to the more abstract—that are geared toward people with developmental disabilities ranging from mild to severe. Some may seem familiar to ones you have created, witnessed or participated in, but they have been modified to most closely meet the developmental and cognitive needs of people with developmental disabilities. It is the responsibility of the facilitator to know the ability of the individual with a disability so to choose a ritual that would be most appropriate and helpful. The rituals can be further modified, individualized, or combined to meet specific needs or can be carried out as they are written.

You will find that these rituals can also be used when people with developmental disabilities experience other significant losses in life. These losses may include (but are certainly not limited to) moving from one living environment to another, graduation or completion of an educational program, or having a family member (parent, sibling, room- or housemate, grandparent, friend) move to a location that makes it more difficult to visit the person with a developmental disability as often as in the past.

For most of the rituals presented, if they are completed prior to the funeral, the finished product (picture, ornament, or letter) can be placed in the casket with the body of the person who died or could accompany the body as it is cremated. The individual with a disability may also want to perform the ritual in the presence of the body. If this is something desired by the individual, it could be done before the other mourners arrive or after they leave. It could also be done in the presence of other mourners.

I invite you to use the rituals contained in this book as a springboard to the creation of new and unique rituals that meet the mourning needs of each unique person with a developmental disability. In helping such a person mourn and heal, you may be "remembering" an otherwise forgotten mourner and enhancing a life forever.

Ritual One

Use of Photographs in Ritual

In brief: Show a photo or photos of the person who has died to the individual with a disability and talk about the person to help the individual mourn the loss. If the individual with a disability is nonverbal, the facilitator can verbalize "for the individual" about the loss.

Materials: A photo or photos of the person who died.

Directions: If the ritual is done in a classroom environment, have the students and others (with and without developmental disabilities) gather in a circle in the classroom, outdoors or in an environment where the students most often interacted with the person who died. Such environments may include the cafeteria if the person who died was a cook at the school or the music room if the person who died was a music teacher.

After the individuals have gathered, pass a photo of the person who died from person to person around the circle. Each person who holds the picture talks about the person while looking at it. Each person could say whatever they are thinking or feeling while looking at the photo. They could also say a word that comes to their mind.

1

If an individual in the circle is unable to verbalize her thoughts and feelings, a person who is able to speak (a facilitator) can "speak for" the individual holding the picture. The facilitator may say something they remember about an interaction between the individual and the person who died. For example, "I remember when Joe (the person who died) helped Elena (the individual with a developmental disability) paint a picture. I also remember Joe and Elena laughing while they painted."

If the ritual is done in a home environment, the gathering could be done at a kitchen table, in a family room or outdoors. Again, each person in the group (with and without disabilities) would take a turn holding the photo and talking about the person who died.

Example: Kari, a student in a high school class for people with severe and profound developmental disabilities, had lived with severe health complications since birth. Most of the students in her class had been together since elementary school and knew each other very well. They were aware of Kari's health difficulties. In February of the year, Kari's health began to deteriorate quickly. She was hospitalized for several days and then she died.

The day following Kari's death, the teacher sat with the students and told them the news. They were all aware that Kari might die soon because the teacher had kept the students updated on Kari's situation. The students, teacher, and assistants cried together and talked about Kari and what she meant to each of them. After the visitation and funeral, which only a few of the students attended, the teacher decided that it might be healing for the entire class to do a ritual at school.

The following morning, the students gathered in a circle. The teacher had a picture of Kari that had been taken for the school yearbook. The teacher invited the students and assistants to take turns holding the photo and saying whatever they wanted about Kari. The teacher started; she held the picture and said, "I will always remember Kari's smile." She passed the photo to a student sitting to her left. The student took the photo and looking at it said, "Friend Kari, friend." The picture continued to be passed around the circle. When it came to Anna, a student who was nonverbal, the teacher sat next to Anna and, as Anna held the picture, the teacher said, "Kari would sit with Anna and laugh." Anna smiled.

After the picture had been passed around the entire circle, the teacher asked if anyone would like another turn to say anything. One student took another turn and then the group sat in silence for a few moments prior to moving away from the circle and continuing on with their day.

Ritual Two

Using Storytelling in Ritual

In brief: Write a story about the person who has died in collaboration with the individual with a disability.

Materials: Paper and writing utensil (pen or pencil) or a computer to write a story about the person who died.

Directions: Write a story about the person who died in collaboration with the individual. After the story is written, read it to and discuss it with the individual. It may be most beneficial to co-write the story with the individual with a developmental disability if she or he is able to assist in the writing. If the individual is unable to assist in the writing, the facilitator can write the story independently.

If the facilitator writes the story independently, it may be helpful for the facilitator writing the story to verbalize his story-writing process while the individual with a disability is present. For example:

"I want to write a story about Kim - let's see - Kim taught at this high school, so I will write 'Kim Jackson taught at Hill High School.' OK, what else? Well, Kim loved her students - in fact I don't know

anyone who loved students as much as Kim did - I'll write, 'Kim loved to see her students each morning. She would stand at the door and say good morning to each student as they came to the room.' OK, that's good. I also need to write about how her students felt about her: 'Kim's students liked Kim, too. They said that Kim was a nice teacher and they learned a lot from her.' Now I want to write about the day that Kim died - that is difficult, but I feel it's important. OK - 'One day, the students came to school, but Kim was not at the door. The students were worried. Jeff Miller was their teacher for the day. He sat down with the students and told the students that Kim was not going to come back to school. He told them that Kim died in a car accident.' Yes, that's what happened. I think I want to write what 'died' means. He said that 'being dead means that Kim's body doesn't work anymore. Kim cannot see or taste or feel anything.'"

It certainly depends on the ability of the individual as to how long and involved the story would be written. This type of story could also be used to describe what the students would see when they attended another ritual, such as a funeral or visitation of the body of the person who died.

Using storytelling in ritual is similar in some ways to "social stories" developed by Carol Gray. However, social stories were created to be used primarily with individuals with autism spectrum disorder. A social story is written with specific guidelines in mind to describe a situation by using cues and typical responses. It is written to ensure that a student has the social information she or he needs, and to present the information so it is easily understood by the student. Using storytelling in ritual is more free-flowing than a social story and has no specific guidelines.

Example: When I was teaching individuals with moderate to severe developmental disabilities at the high school level, one of my students, Marty, experienced the death of his aunt. Marty was verbal and took care of his personal needs independently. He was residing in a group home and was learning to be more independent in the community. His aunt was a primary care provider and Marty had a very close relationship with her. In fact, I always felt that Marty and his aunt had more of a mother-son relationship than an aunt-nephew relationship.

The morning after her death, a staff member from the group home where Marty lived called me. Marty's aunt had died unexpectedly early on a Tuesday morning. The staff member told me that they had talked with Marty about her death, but that he "didn't seem to understand" what had happened. They asked if I could explain the death to Marty. They also asked me to explain the visitation and funeral process so that Marty would be able to attend and not be "surprised" by what he experienced.

After my students arrived that morning and were prepared for the school day, we sat in our "talking circle" and prepared a "story" about Marty's aunt's death, the visitation, and the funeral.

The 12 students sat in an area with a circle of chairs and couches. We used this area for our morning meetings and any time we needed to converse about special events or announcements. First, I told the students that Marty's aunt had died and we talked some about what that meant (her body didn't work any longer, she could no longer hear,

7

see, talk, or feel). The students had varied levels of understanding of death and what happened with ritual after the death. Some of the understanding seemed to be authentic and some seemed to simply be repeating what they had heard others say. For example, one of my students recalled that when her grandmother died, she wasn't able to "handle it." When I asked what she meant by that, she said that she didn't know but that her sister "couldn't handle it, either."

After our short conversation about death, we begin writing a story about Marty's aunt and what would happen at the visitation and funeral. This was done for several reasons. First, the story could help Marty and the other students better understand death and death ritual. Also, the story could be read to Marty when he needed to understand and ritualize the experience.

We started by having Marty tell us about his aunt. He told us what she looked like, what he liked to do with her, and how he felt about her. We then wrote about how his aunt died. The story began, "Marty had an aunt. Her name was Ruth. She was tall and had brown hair. Marty and his aunt liked to talk and watch movies together. Marty loved his aunt very much. One night his aunt went to bed and woke up in the middle of the night with a pain in her chest. Ruth's husband called the hospital to get her some help. The ambulance came to Ruth's house, but the people who came in the ambulance could not help Ruth. Ruth died. Being dead means that Ruth could not move and her body doesn't work anymore. She could not smell, hear, see, or feel."

The story continued by explaining in simple terms what Marty would experience when he attended the visitation and the funeral. I was familiar with Marty and his aunt's religion and could write about what Marty would experience. If I had not been familiar with the death rituals of the religion, I would have needed to contact someone with knowledge of the rituals for that particular tradition.

After writing the story, Marty insisted that Ruth would "get up and make dinner." We spent some additional time talking about the meaning of death and being dead. Marty finally seemed to understand the irreversibility of death. He took the story with him and asked for it to be read to him several times prior to the visitation and funeral. He also had the story read to him daily for several weeks, both at school and at his group home. About a month after Ruth's death, Marty asked for the story to be read on a less frequent basis.

Ritual Three

Use of Memory Objects in Ritual

In brief: Have the people with disabilities put a group of objects together that remind them of the person who has died.

Materials: Objects that belonged to the person who died and objects/pictures that remind the people with disabilities of the person who died

Directions: Have the individual gather objects that belonged to or remind him of the person who died, such as photos of the person who died (with or without the individual with a developmental disability present in the picture), articles of clothing, books, or papers. For individuals with more severe disabilities, it may be important for the facilitator to gather the objects and have the individuals with disabilities pick the ones they want to display from the already gathered objects. The individual then places the objects on a table and says what she or he remembers about the person who died.

If the person with a disability is unable to verbalize her thoughts and feelings, a person who is able to speak (the facilitator) can tell about memories as the person with a disability places the object on the table.

The objects could be left on the table for several days or weeks so the individual can continue to use this ritual in the mourning process. The objects could also be taken down after a short period of time—maybe after a day or even an hour. Limiting the amount of time the objects remain on the table to a short duration may be important if the individual with a disability is easily distracted or tends to fixate on new items in the room. This ritual could also be repeated several times with the same or different objects.

> *Example: Lisa was a 10-year-old with a mild developmental disability. Lisa was taught in the general education fourth grade class and received some additional help from a special education teacher. Lisa's grandmother, Ellen, died one morning. Ellen had been living with congestive heart failure for several years and in recent months had increased difficulty breathing, walking even short distances, and contending with fluid retention. Lisa had a close relationship with her grandmother, but her grandmother didn't talk with Lisa about her illness or the possibility of her death; Ellen didn't feel Lisa would understand.*
>
> *The morning of her death, Ellen called Lisa's mother, Kay, and asked to be taken to the hospital because she "just wasn't feeling very well." By the time Lisa's mother arrived at Ellen's home, Ellen was unconscious. Kay called the ambulance. The ambulance arrived and took Ellen to the hospital; Ellen died en route.*

When Lisa arrived home from school that afternoon, her mother sat with her as Lisa ate a snack, as she did every day after school, and told her Grandma Ellen had died. Lisa started to cry and said that she didn't want Grandma Ellen dead.

Kay decided that it might be healing for Lisa to help create a ritual. Kay and Lisa went to Grandma Ellen's apartment and gathered some objects. Kay told Lisa that she could pick out some things that reminded her of Grandma Ellen. Lisa went to the table by the chair Grandma Ellen usually sat in. Lisa picked up a picture of Grandma Ellen and Lisa that had been taken at Lisa's ninth birthday party. She then went to the kitchen and picked up the coffee mug that Grandma Ellen used. Kay encouraged Lisa to pick several more objects. Lisa picked a scarf, a book, and Grandma Ellen's reading glasses. Kay also picked several objects from the apartment.

Kay and Lisa took the objects home and created a space on a table for the objects to be displayed. As Lisa put the objects on the table one at a time, she talked about why she picked the object, what it reminded her of, and what she would miss about Grandma Ellen. Kay also put the objects she chose on the table one at a time and talked about Grandma Ellen. Kay and Lisa took turns putting the objects on the table.

After the ritual, Kay and Lisa decided to bring the objects to the funeral home for the visitation and display them for the other mourners to see. This also gave Lisa the opportunity to talk with the other mourners about Grandma Ellen and which objects she had picked and what each object meant to her.

Ritual Four

Use of a Plant (or Tree) in Ritual

In brief: Plant a tree or a plant in memory of the person who died and call it the (name of the person who died) _____ memorial/memory/love plant (tree). Talk about the person as you help the individual with disabilities take care of the plant (or tree).

Materials: A plant or young tree. It may be best to use a plant or tree that won't require a lot of "special attention" (such as only a limited amount of sunlight or daily watering). This will better assure that the plant or tree will continue to be a living memorial for the person who died. It may also be helpful to have a picture of the person who died.

Directions: Help, to whatever extent is appropriate, the individuals with disabilities plant the plant or tree. As it's being planted, talk about the person who died and encourage the individual to talk about her memories of the person who died. If the person who died enjoyed gardening or planting, it may be especially meaningful.

After the planting is complete, the individual places a photo of the person who died near the site; if there is a photo of the person who died together with the individual with a developmental disability, this may be especially meaningful to the individual. If the plant or tree is outdoors in an unprotected area, it will be important to make sure the photo is protected. Lamination, framing, or enclosure in a small shelter might be appropriate.

During subsequent caring for the plant or tree, talk about the person who died and again encourage the individual with disabilities to do the same. It may be that the person with a disability will tell the same story each time you care for the plant or tree. Remember that repeated memories also serve as a time of mourning. Also, the individual with a disability may repeat a story he has heard from you or another person. If the individual with a disability is nonverbal, the facilitator may be the only one actually speaking. This may also serve as a time of mourning for the individual.

Some individuals with developmental disabilities may choose to visit the site each day. They may also choose to do a repeated activity, such as sing a song, play some music, or read or listen to a passage or story.

Example: Bitsy volunteered with Jamahl's elementary class of students with moderate developmental disabilities. There were six students in the class and one paid assistant. The students worked on basic academic skills as well as communication and self-help tasks. Ever since her retirement three years before, Bitsy helped in the class two to three days a week. She not only planned but also participated in class parties and other activities.

Jamahl was notified one afternoon that Bitsy had been killed in a car accident the evening before. He waited until the following day to inform the students of Bitsy's death. This gave him time to contact all the parents and inform them of Bitsy's death, talk with the school social worker, Patsy Knoll, about how to talk with the students, and, with Patsy's assistance, plan the ritual for the following morning with the students.

When the students arrived at school the following morning, Jamahl and Patsy told them about Bitsy's death. After the students had a few minutes to respond, Jamahl informed the students that they would be planting a rose bush outside their window so they could remember Bitsy when they looked at it. Roses were Bitsy's favorite flower and she often brought roses to the class when she came to volunteer.

The students went outdoors. Jamahl, Patsy and the teaching assistant helped each student take turns in the planting process—digging the hole, placing the bush in the hole, covering the hole with dirt. Each student in turn was encouraged to talk about Bitsy and what they remembered about her. Several of the students had difficulty verbalizing their thoughts, so one of the facilitators spoke for them (for example, "I remember Bitsy planning the winter party with us this year. She was always good at planning parties and helping us feel happy.").

Each school day, Jamahl and one of the students would care for the rose bush together. During this individual time, they would talk about Bitsy and memories they had of her.

Ritual Five

Use of Drawing in Ritual

In brief: The individual with a disability draws a picture of the person who died and has the opportunity to share the picture and memories with others.

Materials: Paper and some tools to create the picture (marker/colored pencils/crayons/paint)

Directions: Provide the individual with a disability an opportunity to draw a picture of the person who died. The individual may want to draw a picture of an activity she enjoyed doing with the person who died or simply a portrait of the person who died. Even if the individual with a disability has limited fine motor skills and is unable to draw with much or any reality, encourage the individual to draw whatever she remembers (even if it is circles or scribbling). What may appear to be random lines to another person may signify a specific event or portrait to the individual doing the drawing.

The adult can then ask the individual with a disability to "tell about the drawing." The individual can talk about what he is drawing as he draws or after the drawing is complete. If there are several pictures from the same or different individuals, all the pictures can be copied and made into a booklet. The individual can use the booklet to look at or show to others to give them more opportunities for mourning.

A variation of having the individual draw a picture is to make a light copy of a picture of the person who died on a copy machine and have the individual either trace or color the picture. This will give the individual structure while drawing or coloring, which for some people might be more helpful than freehand drawing techniques.

> *Example: One of the students in Marta's third grade class was a young boy named Matthew. Matthew had a mild developmental disability and was integrated into Marta's general education class. He received some additional help with reading and math instruction from a special education teacher; however, Matthew participated in class activities and performed in the average range in most of the subjects. Matthew had three brothers, all older than Matthew.*
>
> *Matthew had a special and close relationship with his grandfather. Matthew's grandfather lived a few miles from Matthew's family and often picked Matthew up after school. Matthew talked about activities that he and his grandfather did on a daily basis. One of Matthew's favorite activities to do with his grandfather was fishing.*
>
> *One morning Marta received a phone call from Matthew's mother telling her that Matthew's grandfather had a stroke and was in the hospital. She also told Marta that Matthew was coming to school and he knew that his grandfather was sick. What Matthew didn't know was that his grandfather's*

stroke was very serious and that he might not live through the day.

Matthew came to school and told Marta and the class about his grandfather being sick and in the hospital. That afternoon, Matthew's mother called and told Marta that Matthew's grandfather had died and she would tell Matthew about the death when he arrived home from school. She also said that Matthew would be out of school for several days for the wake, funeral, and other gatherings.

When Matthew came back to school at the end of the week, Marta greeted him at the classroom door and told him how sorry she was that his grandfather had died. "Oh that's OK," Matthew said. "I had fun. We got to go out and eat and I got to see my uncle." Marta was somewhat concerned about Matthew's casual response, but continued on with the day as usual. That afternoon, the students went to music class with another teacher. Matthew asked if he could stay with Marta rather than go to music. Marta agreed.

When Marta and Matthew were alone in the room, she asked him if he would like to draw a picture of his grandfather; she felt that through drawing Matthew may be able to express his feelings better than through words. Matthew said he would like to draw. Marta told him that he could draw whatever he wanted. He drew a picture of his grandfather and him fishing. He continued by drawing the sun in the sky; the sun was crying. "What a nice picture," Marta told him. "Would you tell me about it?" "Sure," Matthew said. "This is me and Grandpa fishing. I liked to fish with Grandpa, but now I won't be able to do that anymore because he's dead." He pointed at the sun. "The sun is sad that Grandpa is dead and it's crying. It cries a lot. It's very sad. I'm sad, too." Matthew started to cry. Marta sat with Matthew as he cried. She told Matthew that anytime he wanted to talk about his grandfather or draw a picture and tell her about it, he could do so.

Matthew drew one or two pictures each day for the following few weeks. Each time he drew, he would bring the pictures to Marta and tell her about a special time he spent with his grandfather or something he missed. Sometimes Marta would need to give the other students individual work to complete while she and Matthew talked. Other times, Matthew would ask to talk during lunch or recess. After several weeks the drawings and Matthew's need to talk became less frequent.

Ritual Six

Use of Music in Ritual

In brief: The individual with a disability listens to music that the person who died liked or that reminds her of the person who died. This gives the individual with a disability the opportunity to remember and verbalize memories.

Materials: Tapes, CDs, and the equipment to play the music

Directions: The facilitator needs to choose music that was enjoyed by the person who died or music that may remind the individual of the person who died. For example, if the person who died drove a truck, a song about trucks may be appropriate, or if the person who died especially enjoyed listening to country music, a country song could be played.

The music can be played while the individual with a disability is sitting down or lying down. It can be played while the individual with a disability is just listening, or while he is participating in a quiet activity, such as drawing a picture of the person who died, or while doing an activity that the person who died used to do her (perhaps some self-help or functional skill).

While or after the music is played, discuss with the individual how the music makes you, the facilitator, feel and solicit feelings from the individual with a disability. It could be that the person with a disability would only be able to "show the emotion" with facial expressions or may simply repeat what you have said. If the individual with a disability repeats or is nonverbal and can only show the emotion, you could name several possible emotions that the individual may be feeling and have him choose. You could also have some visible representation of emotions (such as line drawings of faces that represent happy, sad, angry...) and have the individual with a disability point to one or more of the symbols that depict how she is feeling. The facilitator may want to elaborate on a choice by verbalizing it. For example: "You pointed to the happy face. The happy face reminds me of the happy times you spent with (the name of the person who died). I remember one time when (the name of the person who died) was playing ball with you and you were both laughing."

Example: Lora was a 14-year-old student with a severe developmental disability. She used a wheelchair for mobility, and needed help from others in moving the chair. She was nonverbal, but did seem to understand emotions, smiled when she saw people she liked, laughed and smiled when music was played, and pointed to "yes" and "no" when responding to a question.

Lora's sister, Maria, was 17 years old. Maria went to the same school as Lora and would come into Lora's classroom several times a week to say hi to Lora and her classmates. Lora always smiled when she saw Maria. When Maria had time, she would sit with Lora, talk with her, and comb Lora's long hair. Lora would smile and laugh while her hair was being combed.

On the way to school one morning, a car hit Maria as she crossed the street. She was in a coma for several days prior to dying. During her hospitalization, Lora was told that Maria was very sick. The day of Maria's death, Lora's mother called the school and asked Lora's teacher, Daniel, to tell Lora about Maria's death. Lora's mother told Daniel that she was too upset to tell Lora herself.

Daniel sat with Lora and told her of Maria's death. Lora seemed to know something was serious, but did not seem to understand about the death. Daniel talked with Lora on an ongoing basis about Maria's death. During each conversation, Lora seemed to listen intently, but did not respond to the news in any particular manner.

A month after Maria's death, Daniel decided to create a ritual with Lora. He talked with Lora about Maria's death and asked Lora if it would be OK if he combed her hair while they listened to some music. Lora pointed to a "yes" card. As Daniel sat with Lora, a song that Lora always seemed to enjoy was playing. He combed her hair and talked about Maria. He remembered how Maria would come into class and sit with Lora and comb her hair. Lora listened intently and after several minutes started to cry. Daniel sat with Lora as she cried. He repeated this activity several times each week for several weeks. Each time he first obtained Lora's permission; she pointed to "no" on two occasions. The first several times Lora indicated that she wanted to participate in the ritual, she cried. After several weeks, Lora didn't cry as much and would smile when she participated in the ritual.

Ritual Seven

Use of Writing in Ritual

In brief: The individual with a disability writes or dictates a letter to or about the person who died.

Materials: Paper and writing utensil or computer

Directions: This ritual may be most appropriate for individuals with mild developmental disabilities. Help the individual with a disability write a letter to the person who died. The letter could be written individually, with assistance from the facilitator, or dictated while having the facilitator write the letter for the individual with a disability. Another way of writing the letter is to have an outline of the letter with sentence starters or sentences with blanks that the individual can complete. For example:

Dear _____,
I feel _____ that you have died.
The times I feel saddest is when I

_____.

What I miss most about you is

_____.

One thing I want to tell you is

_____.

Love, _____

After the letter is finished, the individual could read the letter to others. If there is more than one individual with a disability involved with the letter-writing ritual, the individuals could take turns reading aloud what they have written. If an individual is nonverbal or unable or unwilling to read the letter aloud, the facilitator or other participant could volunteer to read the letter.

If letters are written prior to the funeral, they can be put in the casket with the body of the person who died or cremated with the body. The person with a disability may also want to read the letter in the presence of the body. This can be done prior to the arrival of or after the departure of other mourners at the funeral home or in the presence of other mourners. Some other options for the letter are to have the individual with a disability place it at the gravesite or by the urn, or attach it to a helium-filled balloon or balloons (depending on the weight of the letter) and release it into the air.

Example: Curt was a 13-year-old boy with a mild developmental disability. He was able to do basic academic skills in reading, writing, spelling, and math. He and his cousin, Brad, were the same age and attended the same school. Brad and Curt grew up living a few blocks from one another. Their families spent a lot of time together.

One Saturday, Audrey, Curt's teacher, received a call from Curt's mother, Beth, saying that Brad and his father had been in a car accident. Brad's father was hurt, but would recover. Brad, however, was very badly injured and they weren't sure that he would live. Later that day Beth called Audrey again to tell her that Brad had died that afternoon. Beth told Audrey that she had talked with Curt about Brad's death; Curt was very sad and went to his bedroom and wouldn't come out.

On Monday, when Curt arrived at school, Audrey sat with Curt and talked with him about how he was feeling. "It's not fair that I can't see Brad anymore," Curt told Audrey. "I want to play with him again." He cried. Audrey asked Curt if he would like to write Brad a letter saying how he felt. Audrey explained that even though Brad could not reply to the letter, Curt might like being able to tell Brad how he felt.

Curt sat with a paper and pencil and wrote "Dear Brad" and then sat thinking for a long time. "I can't think of what to write," he told Audrey. Audrey created an outline of a letter for Curt to fill in. She wrote:

Dear Brad,
I feel _____ that you were killed in the car accident. The thing I liked about you was _____. What I will miss most about you is _____.
I love you,

This outline gave Curt the opportunity to write a letter in a structured manner and gave him a lot of support in the writing process. Curt filled in the blanks with the following:

Dear Brad,
I feel very, very, very sad that you were killed in the car accident. The thing I liked about you was you were nice to me. What I will miss most about you is me and you playing.
I love you,
Curt

Curt also put several dog stickers on the letter because he said that Brad liked dogs. Audrey asked Curt what he would like to do with the letter. She gave him several options: he could keep it by putting it in a safe place, he could put it in Brad's casket, or he could keep it in his pocket so he could read it when he wanted to. Curt thought about it and decided to put the letter in an envelope and put it in Brad's casket, so "it would be with Brad for always."

The following evening, at Brad's visitation, Curt brought the letter to the funeral home. He took the letter out of the envelope, read it out loud, put it back in the envelope, and put it in the casket with Brad's body.

Ritual Eight

Use of Stones in Ritual

In brief: Invite the individual with a disability to share a memory about the person who has died then place a small stone in a decorative fountain (she could also paint the stone or write a word or phase on the stone). Have the fountain present in the room. Run it each day and have a time to remember the person who has died.

Materials: Stones and waterproof paint, water fountain

Directions: Gather or purchase stones. If the stones are going to be painted or written on, it may be most effective to find or purchase smooth stones. If you'd like, invite the individual to paint or write on the stones something that he remembers about the person who died. As he places the stones in the water fountain, the individual says (or the facilitator "speaks for the person" who is nonverbal) something he remembers about the person who died. If there is more than one person with a disability involved with the ritual, each individual could take a turn placing a stone and saying something they remember. If there is one individual with a disability involved with the ritual, the individual or facilitator could invite others with and/or without disabilities to participate.

Example: Phyllis was a 22-year-old woman with a mild developmental disability who lived at a group home and had a cleaning job at a local fast food restaurant. She also attended classes to learn additional job skills. Phyllis met Dale, a 25-year-old man with a mild developmental disability, at work. Phyllis and Dale spent time together before and after work talking and taking walks together. Phyllis told people that she and Dale were dating, but Dale would tell her that they were not dating, they were just friends. After several months, Phyllis and Dale started to spend more time together. They would get together at each other's homes for dinner, watching videos, and talking.

One afternoon, while walking to Phyllis' home so they could walk to work together, Dale was crossing the street and was struck by a truck that failed to stop for a stoplight. Dale was killed instantly. Phyllis waited for Dale to arrive. When he didn't show up, Phyllis called his home and was told that he had left over an hour earlier. Phyllis told the group home staff person, Lamar, that she was worried. Lamar contacted the home where Dale lived and together they decided to contact the police and the local hospital. Within an hour they found out that Dale had been killed.

Phyllis was very sad. She stayed home from work the day of Dale's death and spent most of it in her room crying. Phyllis later attended the wake and funeral. The staff at the group home was extra attentive to Phyllis for several weeks after the death; they would sit and talk with her about how she was feeling.

*One weekend, Lamar asked Phyllis if she would like
to do something special to remember Dale. Phyllis
agreed. Phyllis had a small water fountain in her
room that she liked to run in the evening and listen
to the water tumble over the rocks as she fell asleep.
Lamar suggested that they take some of the stones
from the fountain and write words on them that
reminded Phyllis of Dale.*

*Phyllis picked four stones. She used a permanent
marker and wrote one of the following words on
each stone: love, smile, friend, and happy. Lamar
and Phyllis invited the other residents into her room
as they placed the stones back in the fountain. As
Phyllis returned the stones to the fountain, she
talked about Dale and the activities that she and
Dale did together. After all the stones were back in
the fountain, she turned on the water. The other
group home residents one by one spontaneously
hugged Phyllis and some cried with her.*

Ritual Nine

Use of Photos of the Death Process

In brief: Help the individual with a disability view pictures of the person alive and dead.

Materials: Photos of the person who died at different points throughout the dying process

Directions: Have a care-partner take photos of the person who is in the active dying process at different stages of the process (i.e., when the person looks healthy, when the person is close to death, the body after the person dies, the body in the casket...). Make a photo album with the sequence of pictures. The individual with a disability can look at the pictures and talk about the stages of the death process. In cases of sudden death, this ritual can also be done with photos of the person when she was alive and photos of her after she died. This would simply require a photo or several photos of the person's body after death.

Comparing photos from when the person was alive with photos taken after the death may make it easier for people with disabilities to understand what "dead" means and acknowledge the reality of the death. Looking at and talking about the photos may also help them mourn in the days, weeks, months, and even years after the death.

Example: Jennifer was a 14-year-old girl with a moderate developmental disability. She attended a junior high school and received most of her education in a special education resource room. She was very verbal and had friends with whom she ate lunch every day.

Jennifer's grandfather was diagnosed with cancer and was given several months to live. Jennifer's mother, Sarah, talked with Jennifer on several occasions about her grandfather's condition and his impending death. Jennifer did not seem to understand the irreversibility of her grandfather's death. For example, Jennifer would say, "After the funeral, Grandpa and I can go to the store to shop for school clothes."

Sarah decided to document the grandfather's dying and death process with photos in an attempt to help Jennifer understand. Sarah, with permission from Jennifer's grandfather, took pictures of him when he was relatively healthy, progressively more ill, within an hour of his death, his body immediately after his death, his body in the casket, the casket being prepared for burial, the lowering of the casket, and the grave after it had been covered with dirt. Some of the pictures were of the grandfather alone and some were of the grandfather with Jennifer.

Sarah put the photos in an album. She used captions to describe whether the grandfather was alive, dying, or dead. Jennifer was able to look at the album whenever she had the need to see the pic-

tures. She also used the album as a way of mourning the death of her grandfather; she would show the album to friends and relatives. As she showed the album, she would talk about her grandfather, what they did together, what he meant to her and which pictures showed him alive and which pictures showed him when he was dying and dead. This seemed to help Jennifer understand and mourn the death of her grandfather.

Ritual Ten

Use of Space & Location in Ritual

In brief: The individual with a disability is given the opportunity to remember the person who died in the different environments in which she knew the person (home, school, work, etc.).

Materials: Photos of the person who died and access to the environments in which the person with a disability interacted with the person who died

Directions: Pick 3-5 areas where the person who died used to be present for the individual (the living room, the kitchen, the bedroom...). Place a photograph of the person who died in each area. Guide the individual with a disability from one location to the next, inviting him to remember the person who died and the activities they shared together in each space. The facilitator can also verbally remember the person who died.

Example: Paige was a 17-year-old with a moderate developmental disability who attended high school. She was educated in a separate classroom for most

39

of the day. She was integrated into the general education classroom for several classes where she was able to work at her own pace and ability (art class and a self-paced family consumer science class). When she attended the general education classes, she had a volunteer high school student who was her companion and helper. Since the school was large and could be somewhat chaotic as students passed from one class to another, Paige's teacher, Quentin, felt it would be good for Paige to have a chaperone for passing periods.

The student who accompanied Paige to her classes was Carla. Most of the time Paige would lead the way, but there were times when she became confused with the directions and needed Carla to help her find her classroom. As Paige and Carla walked to class, they would talk. Paige became attached to Carla and looked forward to seeing her each day.

One morning Carla didn't show up to assist Paige to her morning art class. Quentin had not heard from Carla; she always called if she was going to be absent so he could arrange for Paige to get to class with another person. Paige was anxious about Carla not showing up. Quentin called the attendance office to find out if they had heard any news about Carla's absence. He was told that there had been a car accident that morning and three students, including Carla, were killed. When he hung up the phone, he sat with Paige and the other students and told them the news. Paige and the other students cried.

As time went on, Quentin found another student to accompany Paige to her general education classes.

Paige said that she liked the new student, but really missed Carla. Quentin decided to create a ritual with Paige. He had a school picture of Carla that she had given him several weeks before her death. He made some photocopies of the picture and pasted them to the wall outside of the art and consumer science classrooms. He told Paige of the pictures and told her that when she went to class that day, instead of going right into class, they would spend some time talking about Carla while looking at the photos.

That day Quentin accompanied Paige to her classes. When they arrived at the art class, they waited until all the other students had gone into the room and spent some time looking at Carla's picture, talking, and crying. When Paige was ready to attend class, they took the picture down and Paige put it in her backpack. That afternoon they did the same thing at the consumer science classroom.

Paige carried the pictures of Carla with her for several weeks. One day she took the pictures out of her backpack and put them on a side table in the classroom. She told Quentin that she was going to the art class with the other student. She continued to look at Carla's pictures in the classroom and after a few months took them home with her.

Ritual Eleven

Use of Daily Objects in Ritual

In brief: The individual with a developmental disability is given the opportunity to mourn when using a mug with a photo of the person who died.

Materials: Mug with a photo of the person who died

Directions: Give each individual with a disability a mug with a picture of the person who has died or a picture of something that would remind the individual of the person who died (e.g., a picture of school, the person's car...). The photo can be permanently affixed on the mug by bringing it to a photo shop and having the image imprinted. Each time the individual with a disability uses the mug, encourage him to share thoughts and memories of the person who died. The cup could also have words that remind the individual of the person who died, such as "friend Beth" or "teacher Lindwood."

Photos can also be printed on other items that the individual could wear or use. For example, a photo could be printed on a button or pin that the individual could wear or words or images could be formed into a bracelet.

Example: Tristan was a seven-year-old boy with a mild developmental disability. Tristan was integrated into the general education class at school and was keeping up with the other students with some extra assistance from the special education teacher. He had three sisters and a brother. All his siblings were older than he was.

His father, Kris, worked as an over-the-road truck driver and would spend as much time with Tristan and his other children as he could when he was home. Tristan would come to school after he spent time with his father and report how much fun they had. Kris would take Tristan for short rides in his truck, which was one of the activities Tristan liked to do most with his father.

Kris was killed one night while driving in another state. Tristan's mother, Misty, told the children of the death as soon as she found out. Tristan seemed upset and asked questions of his mother over and over. "When will daddy come home?" "Will he be able to drive anymore?" "Can we go to heaven to visit him?" It took several days for Kris' body to be brought back to his home state. Misty decided to have Kris' body cremated rather than have a burial. There was a funeral service with Kris' ashes present.

Several days after the funeral, Misty asked the children if they would like to have mugs with their daddy's picture on them; this way the children could remember their father every time they used their individual cups. Tristan and his siblings readily agreed. They sat with their mother and looked through photo albums. Each child picked a picture of their father. Tristan picked a picture of his father standing by his truck. That afternoon Misty brought the pictures to a local photo shop and had each picture imprinted on a cup. The imprinted cups took several days to complete.

Tristan used his mug every morning for breakfast and every evening for dinner. He and his siblings often talked about their father as they looked at the pictures on each other's cups.

Ritual Twelve

Use of Daily Memory in Ritual

In brief: Have the person with a disability participate in a daily activity she used to do with the person who died.

Materials: Whatever materials are needed to complete the daily activity

Directions: Choose an activity that the person who died used to do with the individual and do it with him. In many cases, this is an absolute necessity (such as self-help or self-care activities that the individual with a disability is unable to complete independently). In other cases the activity could be taking a walk, biking, cooking together, or playing a game. As the activity is being done, the facilitator intentionally talks about the person who has died.

This ritual may be started soon after the death of the significant person or delayed for several weeks. It is common for people to mourn in doses rather than continuously. For example, a person may have intense times of mourning followed by periods of less painful grief. Because people mourn in doses, talking about the person who died during every daily activity may not be a good idea.

Pay attention to the person's cues— verbal and nonverbal— about her need to mourn. It is important for the facilitator to be aware of these cues in order to help in the healing process.

Example: Crystal was a 13-year-old student with a moderate developmental disability. Crystal was able to do basic academic work and needed assistance with her self-help tasks.

Lois, a teaching aid who worked with Crystal for several years, died from cancer. Lois had been living with cancer for several years. She kept working, but worked less and less as the cancer progressed. Lois helped Crystal with her personal care activities each morning, such as combing her hair and brushing her teeth. As Lois became progressively more ill and was increasingly absent from school, other teaching aids or the teacher would assist Crystal in her morning self-care routine. Crystal would always talk about how much she missed Lois when anyone else helped her in the morning.

Lois had been gone from school for several weeks prior to her death. After Lois' death, Crystal's teacher told the class that Lois had died. One of the other aids in the class took over assisting Crystal in her morning self-care routine. Each morning, while Crystal was getting ready for the day, her new assistant would talk with her about Lois. Crystal would always tell the new assistant how much she missed Lois and wanted her to come back to school. The new assistant emphasized in every conversation that Lois was not coming back to school because she had died.

After several months of Crystal talking about Lois each morning, she started to talk about her new assistant more often when another aid or teacher needed to assist, Crystal would talk about missing her new assistant, but would always add that she missed Lois, too.

Ritual Thirteen

Use of Packing Up Belongings in Ritual

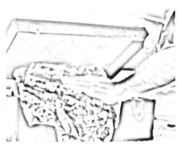

In brief: Pack up the possessions of the person who died and move them to a different space in which the individual with a disability can see the relocation.

Materials: A box or crate in which to put belongings of the person who died

Directions: If the ritual is done in a classroom environment, what is packed may be some books, papers, and contents of a desk or workspace. If the ritual is done in a home environment, clothes and other belongings could be packed. Invite the individual with a disability to assist you in packing all or some of the belongings of the person who died.

As the belongings are being packed, talk with the individual about the person who died and invite him to share memories of the person. Certainly the objects being packed may bring up many memories for the care provider as well as the individual with a disability.

After the box is packed, the facilitator needs to either write the name of the person who died on the box or secure a photo of the person who died to the box. The box can be placed in a space that is visible to people in the room. Leave the box in the space as long as is reasonable; ideally the box or crate should remain until the person with a disability is ready for it to be removed. If, however, the box needs to be removed (because the objects need to be given to another person or it is not reasonable to keep the box in the room), make sure to inform the individual with a disability that the box is going to be removed, when it will happen, and where it is going. If it is reasonable, have the individual with a disability assist in removing the box.

Example: Erick was a 13-year-old student with a severe developmental disability. He was nonverbal, used a wheelchair for transportation, and needed assistance with eating, toileting, and grooming. Charlotte was Erick's teacher and there were also three assistants in the room. No single assistant was assigned to Erick; instead, all the assistants and Charlotte rotated working with all the students. The students, Charlotte, and each assistant had a locker in the room where materials could be kept and coats hung.

One of the assistants, Helen, who had been working with the students for the past six years, had moved with the class as they went from the elementary building to middle school environment. Erick recognized Helen and allowed her to assist him in activities without protest, but he would protest assistance from adults he didn't know well.

Helen had been diagnosed with heart disease and, even though she continued to work at the school,

*started to reduce or eliminate activities that
required exertion. She no longer lifted the students
and after several months, could no longer push
wheelchairs for the students. One day at lunch,
Helen left the cafeteria early and returned to the
classroom. When the other assistants and students
arrived at the room, Helen had already been taken
to the hospital. The next morning, Helen died.*

*Charlotte and the assistants decided to leave
Helen's locker untouched for several weeks. One
day they gathered the students near Helen's locker
and slowly removed the items from the locker and
put them in a box. With the removal of each item,
one of the adults spoke of Helen—what they remembered about her, what they remembered about the
item, or what they missed about her. They were
careful to include stories that involved each of the
students in the class. They also invited the students
who were able to help remove items.*

*The students also participated by sharing memories.
Most of the students in the class were nonverbal, but
those who were able to verbalize recalled some
memories (Helen nice, helped, me miss). After all
the items were taken from the locker, one of the
assistants pasted a photo of Helen on the box and
placed the box on top of the locker where the students could easily view it. Charlotte talked with the
students about how they could look at the box with
Helen's photo whenever they needed to do so.*

*A newly hired assistant later used the locker, but the
box remained on top of the locker for the remainder
of the year. At the end of the year, the box was
taken from the top of the locker and taken out of the*

classroom. Charlotte and the assistants talked with the students about the final removal of the box for several weeks before the end of the school year. When the box was removed, the students and the teachers were again gathered around the locker and together they shared memories of Helen.

Ritual Fourteen

Use of a Pendant or Ornament in Ritual

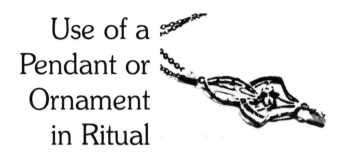

In brief: The individual creates a small pendant that she can wear to remind her of the person who died.

Materials: Clay or some modeling material

Directions: Invite the individual with a disability to create a pendant. Clay or modeling material can be shaped into a representation of the person who died, something that reminds the individual of the person who died, a representation of a feeling (if the individual is able to deal with abstract concepts), or whatever you and the individual decide fosters memories of the person who died. Make sure to make a hole at the top of the pendant so it can be worn on a chain or hung as an ornament.

After the pendant is created, glaze it, if clay is used, and have it fired. If the material used dries on its own (which may be better for some individuals because it is ready to use quickly), invite the individual to paint the pendant or write a word or phrase on it.

After the pendant is finished, attach it to a chain or string so it can be worn or hung as an ornament.

Example: Bella was a nine-year-old girl with a moderate developmental disability. She was integrated into the general education classroom for most of the school day and was able to work at the third grade level with some assistance. She had several friends at school in the general education third grade class. One of her friends was Janna. Janna was not only in Bella's class, she also lived in Bella's neighborhood. Janna came to Bella's house after school several days as week and Bella went to Janna's house after school several days a week.

One day Janna told Bella that Janna's father, Freddie, had cancer and was very sick. Janna said that they would not be able to play at her house anymore because her father needed rest and quiet. Bella felt sad that she wouldn't be able to see Freddie as often as she used to; she liked Janna's father. In the past, when she went to their house, Freddie would play ball with them. He also taught Janna and Bella how to play checkers.

One day Janna didn't show up for school. The teacher told Bella's class that Janna's father had died. After school, Bella went to Janna's house and Janna told her that Freddie had gone to the hospital and died. They both cried.

When Bella went home, her mother talked with Bella about Freddie's death and suggested that they make something that they could look at to remind them of Freddie. Bella and her mother took some quick-drying clay and molded it into a flat oval.

They put a hole at the top of the oval so they could hang it when it was finished.

Bella's mother gave Bella some paints and they talked about what Bella might paint that would remind her of Freddie. Bella and her mother talked about things that Bella liked to do with Freddie. Bella decided to paint some balls on the oval; she always liked playing ball with Freddie. Bella painted several balls of different colors on the oval. They allowed the clay and paint to dry, put a piece of yarn through the hole at the top, and hung the pendant on a corkboard that Bella had in her room. Bella was able to see the pendant every night when she fell asleep and every morning when she woke up. Bella talked about Freddie every day for the first several weeks after his death. She also remembered Freddie and Janna in her evening prayers as she looked at the pendant.

Ritual Fifteen

Use of a Heart Picture in Ritual

In brief: Individuals with disabilities create two heart pictures—one representing themselves and one representing the person who died.

Materials: Construction paper, markers or paints, old magazines, and two photos: one of the person who died and one of the person with a disability

Directions: The facilitator finds or makes two large hearts from oversized construction paper or butcher paper. The hearts can be light red or whatever color seems appropriate (perhaps the favorite color of the person who died or a color that is significant to the individual with a disability). The photo of the person who died is then pasted into the center of one heart and the photo of the individual with a disability is pasted into the center of the other heart.

Next, the individual with a disability is invited to write, draw or choose images from magazines that remind him of the person who died (these go on the heart with the photo of the person who died) and capture his feelings about the death (these go on the heart with his photo). If the individual with a disability does not have enough fine motor ability to draw or write, the facilitator can do the writing, drawing and cutting and pasting. Invite the individual with a disability to circle or point to the images that feel most significant. If the individual with a disability is verbal, she could talk about why the images are significant.

Example: Florence and Carrie both had mild to moderate developmental disabilities. They had gone to elementary, junior high, and high school together. Shortly after high school, they moved into a semi–independent living environment together; they cared for themselves with the assistance of staff who were available each day.

Florence and Carrie lived together for 17 years. In that time, not only did they become more independent and only needed staff to check in on them several times a week, but they also became very close friends and would spend most of their free time together.

On a routine doctor's visit for a yearly physical, Carrie was diagnosed with ovarian cancer. She underwent treatment. Florence was with Carrie during every doctor's visit and would take care of her at home when Carrie wasn't feeling well. The treatments seemed to help, but during a check-up Carrie learned that the cancer had spread to other parts of her body and her life expectancy was short.

Florence and Carrie would talk about Carrie dying and cry together. When Carrie died, Florence's input was used to help make the funeral arrangements. The evening after the funeral arrangements were made, Geoffrey, a staff worker who had known Florence and Carrie for many years, suggested that

Florence create some pictures that could be displayed at the wake and funeral service. Geoffrey cut out two hearts from construction paper. One was green, Florence's favorite color, and one was blue, Carrie's favorite color. Florence pasted a photo of Carrie on the blue heart and a photo of herself on the green heart. Around the picture of Carrie she wrote words and drew picture that reminded her of what Carrie liked and was like (happy, friend, nice, clowns, motorcycles, ketchup...). Around her own picture she wrote and drew pictures of how she was feeling (sad, happy to have Carrie as my friend, loved...).

Florence took the hearts with her to the wake. She put the hearts in the casket on Carrie's body by her hands. Many of the other mourners talked with Florence about the hearts with the words and pictures. This gave Florence additional opportunities to mourn with others.

Ritual Sixteen

Use of Light in Ritual

In brief: The individual with a disability turns on a light to illuminate photos or objects that are reminders of the person who died.

Materials: A light or electric candle and photos and/or objects that are reminders of the person who died

Directions: The facilitator and the individual with a developmental disability set up an area with photos and/or some objects that were owned by the person who died or simply remind the individual with a developmental disability of him or her. This creates a tableau, or a sort of memory table. The area should have a light or electric candle set up so, when it is turned on, it will illuminate the photos and/or objects. The facilitator can invite the individual with developmental disabilities to turn on the light and talk about what she remembers about the person who died.

Whenever the individual with a developmental disability wants to have time with the tableau, he can turn on the light and sit or stand near the objects. The individual could also opt to have a facilitator come with him so he could verbalize his thoughts and feelings to a listener and have another person physically close by for support. There could also be a time each day set aside for the individual with developmental disabilities to turn on the light and actively remember the person who died.

Example: Hallie was an 11-year-old girl with a mild developmental disability. She received most of her education in a resource room with other children with developmental disabilities, but was also integrated into the general education classroom for several subjects. Hallie and her friends and fellow classmates, Kizzy, Laticia, and Tisha—all of whom had developmental disabilities—would eat lunch together and play with one another during recess.

The girls had several teachers they saw each day. One of the teachers was Leonard. He taught them reading and writing. Hallie liked Leonard and some days would arrive at school early so she was able to talk with him before the other students arrived. Hallie also had Linda and Jen as teachers.

One morning when Hallie came to school, Jen and Linda were in the classroom, but Leonard was not there. Both Jen and Linda were crying. Hallie left the room and found Laticia. Hallie told Laticia about how she saw Jen and Linda crying and that Leonard was not at school. When the bell rang, the students sat at their desks. Linda come into the room and talked with the students about how Leonard had died the night before. She told them that he was riding his motorcycle and went off the road. Hallie and the other students felt very sad. Linda talked with them for a long time answering all the questions the students had about Leonard and his death.

After the funeral, another teacher came to the school to replace Leonard. Hallie liked the new teacher, but she cried almost every day, saying that she missed Leonard. About a week after Leonard's death, Linda brought a photo of him to school along with a small lamp. She placed the photo and the lamp on a small table. She had all the students and Jen gather around the table to talk about Leonard and what they remembered and missed about him.

Before anyone spoke, Linda turned the light on so that it shone on Leonard's picture. Each student and teacher spoke about things they liked about Leonard and what they missed. Linda also talked about how the light made it easier for them to see the photo and how, when the light was turned on and they looked at the photo, it might also be easier for them to remember and think about Leonard. After everyone had an opportunity to say what they wanted, Linda told the students that any time they felt sad or wanted to remember Leonard in a special way, they could come to the table, turn the light on and think about him.

Hallie went to the table a lot during the first few weeks. Sometimes she went alone and sometimes she asked one of her friends to accompany her. Jen and Linda also modeled turning on the light and looking at the photo. The photo and the light were left on the table the rest of the year. As the months went on, the students and teachers used the ritual less often.

Ritual Seventeen

Use of Burying an Object in Ritual

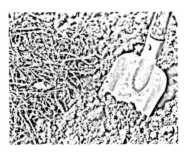

In brief: The individual with a disability buries an object that belonged to the person who died. While burying the object, the individual recalls memories of the person who died.

Materials: An object that was previously owned by or used by the person who died (an article of clothing, a frequently used cup or plate, a piece of jewelry)

Directions: Invite the individual with a disability to create a burial of an object that was previously owned or used by the person who died. The object could be placed in a box, wrapped in a cloth or buried without any covering.

In preparing or picking out the object, the facilitator and the individual with a disability talk about the person who died and what he or she did with the object while alive. Prior to or as the object is being buried, the facilitator talks with the individual with a disability about how, like the object, the person who died will no longer be with them physically, but will remain with them in memory. Continue to talk about the person and the object during and after the burial. If the person with disabilities is nonverbal, the facilitator can verbalize for the person about the loss. A photo of the person or the object being buried can be used as a marker for the burial site.

A time for remembering could be created once a week or on another time interval for the individual with a disability to spend time at the burial site. At these times, the individual with a disability, the facilitator, or both could talk about the person who died, read a letter written to the person who died or play some special music.

> *Example: Topher was a 12-year-old boy with a mild developmental disability. He was integrated into the general education sixth grade class for most of the day. He received instruction in reading, math, writing, and spelling in a resource room setting. His mother left him shortly after his birth and his grandmother, Loretta, was raising him.*

> *Topher's 17-year-old cousin Wesley had lived with them for the past five years. Wesley and Topher did some activities together, such as watching television, playing games, and biking, but most of the time Wesley spent in his bedroom with his door closed. Loretta told Topher that Wesley felt sad a lot.*

> *One afternoon when Topher arrived home from school, police were at the house and his grandmother was talking with them. When Topher's grandmother saw him, she left the conversation with the police officer and sat down with him. She started to cry and said that Wesley had died that afternoon. She said that he died from a disease that made him very sad; it was called depression and he died from suicide. Topher asked about what it meant for*

Wesley to be dead and his grandmother explained it to him.

That evening Topher stayed with his grandmother's friend Lilly while Loretta make arrangements for the funeral. Many people were at the house over the next few days, and Topher attended the visitation and the funeral.

The day after the funeral, Loretta suggested that Topher and she remember Wesley by doing a special activity. She suggested that they bury one of Wesley's shirts in the backyard. Topher picked out a shirt that he liked and that reminded him of Wesley. Together they placed the shirt in a small plastic box. They dug a hole and placed the box in the hole. As they covered the hole with dirt, Loretta talked with Topher about how, just like the buried shirt they could not see any longer, Wesley was also gone and they would not be able to see him any longer. They talked about what they would miss about Wesley. Loretta staked a photo of Wesley, which she had had laminated at a local copy center, into the ground over the burial site. She suggested to Topher that whenever he wanted to remember Wesley in a special way, he could go to the yard by the photo and think about him.

Topher and Loretta went to the burial site together many times over the next few months. At times, Toper picked some flowers and placed them next to the photo.

Ritual Eighteen

Use of a Memory Gift in Ritual

In brief: The individual with a disability symbolically gives a gift to the person who died. The gift represents something the individual will miss about the person who died.

Materials: An object that is owned by or used by the individual with a disability or a drawing or photo that reminds the individual of what she will miss about the person who died

Directions: Invite the individual with a disability to decide on an object she owns or uses that reminds her of what she will miss about the person who died. The individual could also create an object or a picture that reminds her of what she will miss.

The object then becomes a gift for the person who died. The individual places the gift on a table, at the gravesite, or, if the body of the person who died is not yet buried, in the casket. As the individual places the gift, he says something like, "I am giving (name of the person who died) this gift because it reminds me that I will miss..."

If the gift is placed somewhere that is accessible to the individual, a time for remembering what is missed could be created once a week or on another time interval. At these times, the individual with a disability, the facilitator, or both could talk about the person who died, read a letter written to the person who died or play some special music. If the individual with a developmental disability is nonverbal, the facilitator can "speak for" the individual about the loss.

Example: Zoe was a 17-year-old young woman with a moderate developmental disability. She attended high school and was educated in a class for students with moderate developmental disabilities. She also worked at a local fast food restaurant. At the restaurant she worked with several other high school students, some with and some without disabilities.

One worker she know was Alexander, an 18-year-old young man without a disability who was very friendly and helped Zoe learn new skills while she worked (washing the floor, filling the napkin holders, filling needed supplies). Zoe would also see Alexander at school. He invited her to eat with him and some of his friends each noon. Zoe met other high school students through Alexander.

One spring evening while Alexander was swimming at a local lake with some friends, he swam out too far in the lake and was unable to swim to shore. He drowned. Zoe heard the news when she went to work the next afternoon and she was very sad.

Sheree, a young woman Zoe met through Alexander who had been at the lake when Alexander drowned, sat with Zoe at work as Zoe cried. Sheree suggested that they do something for Alexander. She asked Zoe if they could pick a gift for Alexander that reminded them of how much he meant to them and put it in his casket. Zoe and Sheree talked about what they might give Alexander. Zoe decided that she would like to give Alexander a pair of rubber gloves. This reminded Zoe of how much Alexander had helped her learn new skills at the restaurant (they had always worn such gloves when they were cleaning). Zoe asked the manager of the restaurant if she could take a pair of gloves to put in his casket. The manager agreed.

The evening of the visitation, Zoe and Sheree arrived early so they had some time with Alexander's body before others arrived. Sheree had checked with Alexander's parents to get permission for them to spend some time alone with Alexander's body. Zoe put the gloves in the casket next to Alexander's body. Sheree and Zoe talked about what they would say when they put the gifts in the casket. As Zoe put the gloves in the casket, she said, "Alexander, I am giving you this gift because it reminds me of how much I learned from you at work. I will miss you because you were my friend and you liked me." Sheree also put a gift in the casket and said why she was giving Alexander the gift and what she would miss about him. They both cried.

Ritual Nineteen

Use of Play-Doh in Ritual

In brief: The individual with a disability creates a symbol of himself and a symbol of the person who died—putting the two symbols together to represent how they cannot be totally separated from one another.

Materials: Two different colors of Play-Doh. The Play-Doh can be store-bought or homemade. If you'd like to make it yourself, try this recipe:
- 1 cup all purpose flour
- 2 tsp cream of tartar
- 1 tbsp oil
- 1/2 cup salt
- 1 cup water
- food coloring

Mix all dry ingredients together. Add oil, water, and food coloring. Mix dry and wet ingredients together thoroughly. Microwave on HIGH for 3 to 4 minutes, stirring every 30 seconds. Let cool and knead. Store in an airtight container after it's cooled and when not in use.

Directions: Invite the individual with a disability to use one color of the Play-Doh to create something that would represent herself. This could be something she enjoys doing, a model of her body, an object she likes or something she wants to be. With the other color Play-Doh, have the individual create something that represents the person who died.

After the two creations are complete, invite the individual to "smoosh" the two sculptures together. The two shapes and colors can be kneaded together until the original forms are lost and the two colors have become a third color. When she has finished combining the two colors, talk about how the combined colors cannot be separated because they are now one piece of Play-Doh. Talk about how this is like the person who died and the individual with a disability. They cannot be separated from one another because they are part of each other. Now ask the individual to create a final sculpture with the "new" Play-Doh of something that she remembers about the person who died. Talk again about how the new sculpture represents how, even though the person who died is no longer present physically, he or she will always be part of the individual's life.

The new sculpture can be placed so that the individual is able to see it daily. A time can be set aside each day or each week to look at the sculpture. During this time, the individual can talk about the person who died, music can be played, or the individual can remain silent.

> *Example: Thomas was a ten–year-old boy with a moderate developmental disability. He was integrated into the general education fourth grade class most of the day. He did receive some academic support from the special education teacher, Austin, each day for an hour. Thomas lived with his mother, Bonnie, and his father, Greg. His mother had had emphysema for three years and used oxygen in order to breathe.*
>
> *Thomas and his mother were very close and he often talked with Austin about how worried he was that she might die. One afternoon Austin came to Thomas' general education classroom and told*

Thomas that Bonnie had gone to the hospital and was very sick. Thomas' father arrived at the school and took Thomas to the hospital to visit with his mother. Bonnie told Thomas that she was going to die fairly soon; they talked about what that meant and they cried.

Thomas visited his mother in the hospital every day after school. One morning when Thomas came to Austin's room for reading, Austin suggested that they do an activity instead of reading that day. Austin had the other students in the group go with one of the other teachers so he and Thomas could work alone.

Austin had several cans of colored Play-Doh and asked Thomas to pick one of the colors to make something that reminded him of his mother and one color to make something that reminded him of himself. Thomas picked green for his mother and he picked yellow for himself. Austin asked Thomas to create a sculpture that represented his mother out of the green Play-Doh. Thomas created a square pan because, he said, his mother loved to bake. Austin also asked him to create a sculpture that represented himself out of the yellow Play-Doh. Thomas created a book because he liked it when his mother read to him. They talked more about the sculptures and about what he and his mother meant to each other.

After they talked, Austin asked Thomas to take the two sculptures and smoosh them together. Thomas did what he was asked to do.

"Can you take the green and yellow apart again?"
Austin asked.

"I don't think so," Thomas replied. "They are really together."

"This is like you and your mom." Austin told him. "She is part of you and you are part of her, so you will always be with each other even when she has died."

"We will never really be apart?" Thomas said.

"That's right," Austin answered.

Thomas deiced to leave the new combined pieces of Play-Doh at school. Each morning he looked at the Play-Doh and talked about how he and his mother would always be in each other, even after she died. A week later Bonnie died. Thomas took half of the combined Play-Doh to put in the casket alongside his mother's body. "This will help remind her when she is in heaven," he told Austin.

Use of Food in Ritual

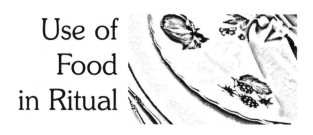

In brief: The individual with a disability helps prepare, serve, and eat foods that either remind the individual of the person who died or are favorites of the individual.

Materials: Food that is chosen by the individual, perhaps with assistance from the facilitator depending on the abilities of the individual. Also needed are the utensils necessary for preparation and serving of the food.

Directions: Invite the individual with a disability to choose foods that represent the person who died or that the person who died enjoyed. If such foods are unknown or the foods would be difficult to prepare, favorite foods of the individual can be chosen.

The individual and facilitator will prepare the foods. If the individual and the person who died prepared food together, it may be good to prepare the foods in the same or similar area. As the food is being prepared, invite the individual to talk about memories of the person who died.

Once the food is prepared, the facilitator and the individual can serve the food to others (some possible participants in the meal could be mutual friends or work partners, family members, fellow students, or teachers; this would depend on the setting in which the ritual is taking place). If the food is served to others, the individual and facilitator should eat with the others. The food could also be served to just the individual and the facilitator.

While eating the meal, the individual, facilitator and others share memories about the person who died, talk about what the person who died meant to them, and describe what they miss about the person. If it does not come up in conversation, the facilitator can talk about how the person who died used to eat and enjoy food, how it is part of life and necessary for life to continue, and how we can remember the person when we eat and continue to live.

Example: Bradley was a 17-year-old young man with a moderate developmental disability. He was educated in a classroom with other students with developmental disabilities. He was able to do self-help tasks independently and worked part-time cleaning at a hospital. He lived with his father, his mother, and one brother and a sister. Both of his siblings were younger than Bradley.

Bradley's father, Caleb, would go on a big hunting trip each year with several friends. When he arrived home, he would prepare whatever he had shot and have a large gathering of friends and family for dinner. Bradley loved the dinner each year. He would tell Caleb that it was better than Thanksgiving.

One year Caleb went hunting with his friends; the second night they were gone, Bradley's mother, Hilda, came to Bradley's room and told him that she had just learned that Caleb had been killed in a hunting accident. The next few days were busy with arrangements for the funeral. Bradley was present with Hilda during the arrangements.

Several weeks after his father's death, Bradley told Hilda that he really missed the annual feast. Hilda suggested that they have the dinner in honor of his father. She invited friends and family as in the past and Bradley helped plan and prepare the meal. Bradley also helped serve the food. Before people began to eat, they talked about how this meal was in honor of Caleb and how much they missed him. During the dinner, people told stories of Caleb. People both laughed and cried.

Every year, Bradley and Hilda continued to prepare a meal as a ritual to honor Caleb. They invited friends and family to attend.

Final Thoughts

Yes, even when individuals with developmental disabilities are forgotten in the mourning process, they grieve and need opportunities to mourn. They need opportunities to participate and heal by the use of rituals specifically created to meet their unique needs. As facilitators, we have the privilege to assist individuals with disabilities during one of the most important and difficult times in their lives. We have the opportunity to help individuals with disabilities heal from the death of a significant person. This is truly an honor. Thank you for your dedication to help people with developmental disabilities mourn well so they can continue to live well and love well.